Kirtland's Warbler

by Richard Rensberry

illustrated by Linda Faith Widing

This book is dedicated to the Kirtland's Warbler Festival of Roscommon, Michigan.

The Kirtland's Warbler

Her nest is a haven

of interlaced grasses

where she lays

        pink eggs

'neath jack pine

        branches.

She has a breast of gold
and a heart with wings,

she grooms her

                feathers

as she chirps and sings.

She feeds on crickets
and firefly flickers,

siphons rain water

from yellow lady

         slippers.

She hatches furry

chicks

with bald blue heads,

teaches them to wobble

and gobble when fed.

Flutters them relentless

in sun drenched sky,

remembers icy winters

and bemoans

       they should fly.

Leaving Roscommon

beneath stars

full bright,

they promise to return

on a warm spring night.

The End

Glossary:

haven- a safe place

interlaced- woven, joined together
                   overlapping fingers

'neath- short for beneath, under

grooms- combs and cleans

siphons- pulls out like through a straw

relentless- not stopping, continuous

drenched- completely covered
                   with something

bemoans- begs for something

In the woods of Lewiston, Michigan
I found my passion of drawing
wildlife in rapid sketch style.

I add another dimension to my
sketches by creating a unique
background for each animal.

By manipulating the light, shadow,
props, and photography, I
capture an illusion of their
environment, and bring the
animals to life!

The process has become a
trademark of my animal
sketches.

Linda Faith Widing

Kirtland's Warblers

Her nest is a haven
of interlaced grasses
where she lays pink eggs
'neath jack pine branches.

She has a breast of gold
and a heart with wings,
she grooms her feathers
as she chirps and sings.

She feeds on crickets
and firefly flickers,
siphons rain water
from yellow lady slippers.

She hatches furry chicks
with bald blue heads,
teaches them to wobble
and gobble when fed.

Flutters them relentless
in sun drenched sky,
remembers icy winters
and bemoans they should fly…

Leaving Roscommon
beneath the stars full bright,
they promise to return
on a warm Spring night.

Richard Rensberry, 4/15/25

Check out many more children's

and adult books

by Author, Richard Rensberry

on Amazon.